# Turn Your Family Around with Laughter

## 12 Steps to Family Joy

### ELISE M. HITTINGER

Printed in the United States of America.

First printing, 2021.

ISBN 978-1-7363195-1-2

www.elisehittinger.com

Editor: Melissa Denelsbeck

# Disclaimer

After a lot of trial and error, the author is giving you the best process from her perspective. The author accepts no responsibility or liability of any kind for any actions or consequences as a result of using the information within this book, whether or not this is in any way due to any negligent act. No guarantees of success are made. The author acknowledges that everyone's circumstances are different, everyone's past is different, everyone's family is different, and the reader assumes responsibility if they choose to use any of the information contained herein. This book is general in nature and is provided for informational purposes only and is not warranted for content, accuracy or any other implied explicit purpose. This book does not provide professional advice and is not in any way recommended as individual advice. The reader should obtain their own independent advice. References to internet sites in this book shall not be construed to be an endorsement of the internet sites, the companies or organizations represented by the internet sites or of the information contained thereon, by the author, publisher or associated parties.

A huge thank you to my wonderful parents, Timothy and Ruth Morehouse, for being the best parents a child could ever have dreamed of and including us in your amazing life!

# Table of Contents

# Foreword

By: Cate Leach

When I was a mere six days old my best friend Elise Marie Morehouse was born. Her family lived across the street from us. While we lived on the same street, had our age in common and both came from large families, the commonalities stopped there. I came from a somber home, with bitterness and anger taking center stage. Time spent in the Morehouse home was filled with love and laughter. Practical jokes that never failed to shock me and parents that took time to get to know me was a constant in my life.

What Elise has written here is the true story of how she was raised by the sweetest, kindest, most generous mom and the full of fun and vigor Dad, both of whom always had a smile, even for the neighbor kid who spent a remarkable amount of time in their home and on their boat. Whether making sandwiches with Fritos inside or making up ridiculous games to pass time in the car, Elise and I are bonded as only friends that literally grew up together can be.

I never witnessed her parents fight. I never heard a harsh word from either of them. I do have a memory of Mr. Morehouse being ill one day, and Elise and I were told to play quietly. It made a memory, because it was so out of the norm!

This book is presented to you in a highly actionable form. You are encouraged to follow in the author's parents footsteps and purposely create the family of your dreams. In a time of chaos and upheaval in our culture, this book is a timely reminder and manual on how to make your home and family a haven for living and dealing with whatever life throws your way.

Perhaps, your family also will take in neighboring waifs who need to experience what family life is meant to be. As an outsider welcomed into the Morehouse home, I see now as a mom of seven myself what a profound impact my time with them had on me. And on my future parenting.

The example the author shares about possessing a willingness to be flexible with rules is one I adopted in my own child-raising. I learned to respond to each child as an individual, recognizing their own unique needs. In reading through the manuscript, I made connections I had missed in the daily life of growing up in and around the Morehouse family. Simple things, like how they taught their children from an early age how to tune into their bodies.

The practical tips shared here, in how to add joy into the family are worth the price of the book, alone. I was blessed to have this remarkable family as my "second" family. The Morehouse family influence was profound and a true Godsend.

# Introduction
A Joyful Family as Seen Through the Eyes of a Child.


I hear so many tragic stories around me of other people's childhoods, and sometimes, I feel like I grew up on another planet. I hear my friends struggling in their families, in their marriages, with their children. I hear the stress, the chaos, the sadness, and the hope in their voices. I hear the challenges of parents, with emotional and physical health of their family. My heart goes out to my friends and their families.

I look back at my childhood and realize that I was extremely lucky, but what can I do to help others? And then it came to me. I can take what I learned growing up, about parenting, families, and joy, and share it in a way that helps others create a vision for their family and a plan to make it happen. They can put the plan in place and enjoy that family they always dreamed of. They can take some of the ideas from my childhood, the ones that feel right, and create that joy and love in their family!

I put together the journey our family went on in a way that others can use to develop their own journey to their dream family. It is possible. It requires a dream of a joyful family and a decision to make it happen. It takes courage to dream of a different life and make it happen. Most of all, enjoy the journey of building the family you have always wanted.

I am going to share the story of my family from the eyes of a child, the view I had of the family growing up, my perspective of an amazing family.  It was not always easy.  It was not always happy.  But I look back and remember it was almost always fun.

Dinner was my favorite time of the day.  When we sat down together at the dinner table, we knew someone was going to their room or going to have to do the dishes, as "punishment" for hysterical laughter.  This was a given.  We would start our dinner with a blessing and passing the food.  This is usually where things would start to go awry. Someone would ask for the butter.  Somehow, the butter was always in front of my dad.  He would pick it up and pass it, and if we were not on guard, as we reached for the butter, he would drop the dish, just enough that we would stick our little fingers, right into the butter.  That would be the start.  A snicker here, a guffaw there, a snort would eventually creep in and then full-blown laughter.  We would gather our wits and continue dishing up dinner.

This was just the start of our dinner time.  As dinner progressed, someone would be eating their mashed potatoes and find a piece of licorice hidden in the midst.  This would start the chuckling all over again.  Someone would be sipping their milk and come across an onion piece floating there.  More laughter.  In order to finish dinner, at some point, my dad would declare, the next person to laugh has to do the dishes (or go to their room, depending on the night).  You have never seen faces so screwed up, determined not to let out a peep of laughter.  Almost every time, it was my mom that would finally let loose with a huge burst of laughter, and she would get sent to her room or have to do the dishes.  Other nights, we would get laughing so hard, we would end up lying on the floor because our sides hurt so bad, we just couldn't sit in the chair any longer.  My memories of dinner together are precious.

I also remember going to friends' houses for dinner. It was so foreign. There were bits of laughter here and there but not the kind that had milk coming out my nose. I could see the difference between the families, and I could definitely see the old adage, laughter is the best medicine.

Our childhood was not perfect to other people's standards, but to me, it was a perfect childhood. I am not sure my siblings would agree, but I do think they would all agree we were blessed to have our mom and dad as our parents. I tell the story about our dinner time, and there are a lot of people that are shocked; it isn't for everyone, but it was perfect for us. It isn't about doing what we did, but it is about creating what is right for you, for your family, to feel that joy and love that we felt as a family.

When I talk to my mom, now in her nineties, we often talk about how blessed we are as a family to have had the joy and the love all rolled into a life that revolved around fun. My biggest concern as a kid was what the next prank would be and on whom that prank would be played. There was no fear of consequences other than the occasional prank that went sideways and got me instead of the intended victim.

My mom and dad now sit on the couch and reminisce about their amazing lives. They are able to cherish these memories as they enjoy their sunset years. They get to remember those days of fun, of laughter, of family, of friends, and all that went into raising five children. We were more like school friends than offspring. Can you imagine growing up as "one of the gang" in a family that was friends. I don't have to imagine; I was one of the gang.

My mom and dad were blessed to have known each other from elementary school as adversaries, which grew into friendship and then grew into love. I believe this is the way relationships should grow, minus the adversary part.

My mom and dad both expressed their emotions, all of them at full volume. We loved, laughed, and cried together. We knew we were loved; we were told we were loved; we were shown we were loved. They also showed us that they loved each other; we saw hugs and kisses between them, a touch here and there, the sparkle in their eyes. They were an example of holding hands, sometimes swinging us between those hands as we took a walk. I know that makes me one of the luckiest kids alive to have open emotions welcomed, all of them - the highs and the lows.

I decided to write my parents' story, from my younger self's perspective. I know so many parents struggling because they didn't have amazing childhoods and may not know how to do things a little different with their children. They were not shown how to be as much a friend to their kids as a parent. My childhood was filled with balance, parenting and friendship, equally. I hope to share some really cool things that can be incorporated into parenting that will give children and parents a chance to create their own magical family.

I never had children of my own to show this to, so I decided to put it into a book so that maybe, through reading this, you can pass on a little of my parents to your children. Give your children a little of the blessings my parents gave to me. I have put together a process to build from where you are to the family you have always dreamed of being, filled with the stories from my own childhood.

Join me on this journey as you walk with me through my childhood. See how many things resonate with you and how they would bring joy to your family. Highlight them or jot them down, so when you finish the book, you can see what your family could look like. I have listed all of the steps in the back of the book, so you have a consolidated place to create your dream family.

# Part 1

# Foundation - What Does a Happy Family Look Like?

# Chapter 1

# The Parents All the Kids Wanted for Their Own

They showed us how to live a life of joy.

Once upon a time, oh wait, this is real! My parents grew up during difficult times; in fact, my mom was born in September the year the market crashed. Can you imagine having that held over your head? Talk about something that could mess up a person! My mom never batted an eye. My dad was a year older than my mom, but they seemed to gain strength from the challenges.

Mom was the youngest of three girls, and her family definitely had some quirks. I may not get the details exactly right, you know, kids glasses and adult memory, but I will give you the best I can recollect of the stories because they are the foundation that no matter how hard a childhood, parents can enjoy being parents.

My mom's mom had to walk to work at the laundry, and her father was not the best financially, a jack-of-all-trades and a master of none. I could feel the struggle financially when my mom talked about her family, lots of pawning and reclaiming of things going on to make it to the end of each month. There were things that had to have been difficult with the great depression, but it also seemed like a lot of love was around them.

When her father passed away, his mistress showed up with two boys, my mom's half-brothers, and my grandmother welcomed the three of them in. They became one large family to try and make ends meet during very rough times until the "other" family got back on their feet. I cannot even imagine this level of kindness. My grandma had the strength of ten women. My mom inherited that strength and her kindness.

My dad's story always gets him to light up in the eyes, and you can see the prankster shine right through as he talks about his childhood. His mom was definitely a roaring twenties gal, and his dad died way too young. He and his brother and their friends were the gang that turned the town upside down and sideways. The stories were of things that most people would just say, "no way, that never happened," but then living with him, I believe every one of them!

We lived in a town outside of Los Angeles that had really steep windy hills all around us. My dad told us stories of taking go carts (the homemade variety) up to the top, and they would just scream down the hills, in and around the cars that were driving up and down the hills. This was just one of the many stories of my dad's childhood.

My dad and his friends could play any prank, on any person, at any time, and somehow, my dad not only lived to talk about it, I don't think he was ever in trouble, or at least not that he admitted. Everyone that met my dad loved him; it is just the way it was. Can you imagine if we could say that about every person we meet? For my world, and the world of my friends growing up, it was that way.

My mom and dad didn't get off to a great start. As the story goes, my dad and his friend, Ernie, used to tell Ernie's dog, Trixie, to chase my mom when she walked home from school, scaring my mom tremendously, so much so that she chose to walk through the vacant lot with the rattlesnakes instead of walking past where the boys were waiting for her with the dog. It turned out the dog would have licked her and just wanted to be loved on, but my mom didn't know that at that time.

Eventually, my mom won over my dad, or my dad won over my mom; they never would admit which one did the winning. I know, without a doubt, they both won. He started carrying her books home from school, and they became friends. They grew up together, pranks and all. My mom talks about the very first dance she went to with my dad. She got all dolled up and wore these amazing high heels. It turned out that they walked to the dance and back, and even though my mom had a great time, she remembers that was the last time she ever wore heels! Could be why I stick to flats, so I don't repeat her mistake!

My dad joined the Navy, and they decided they would date others and broaden their experiences while my dad was away. I know my mom stayed in touch with her "beau" from during that time, and I even got to meet him once, but nobody held her heart like my dad did. Apparently, she held his heart too.

My dad, being the joker that he is, sent my mom a letter with the words "Will you marry me?" all scrambled up. When he called to talk to her on the phone, he asked if she knew what he wrote, and she said there was no way she could figure that out. She later admitted that there was no way she was going to say "Will you marry me?" to him; he would hold it against her for the rest of her life, and we all know, that was absolutely true!

I am so grateful that my dad finally did ask my mom to marry him because that was the beginning of our family!

They were blessed to grow up together and get married while still having that "kid" attitude and friendship. They lived their life in this place of deep friendship first and foremost, and the family just came along for the ride. My mom says they were kids, they got married, and added more kids to the gang. That is sure what it felt like to me and all my friends too!

They had many struggles I am sure, but they never really talked about them much. When they were first married, I know my mom wanted to talk one night, and my dad went to sleep, so my mom slapped him. He just got up and left for a few days, and when he came back, they never spoke of it; they just forgave each other and went back to friendship. This was shared with me when I was going through a really rough time, and my mom shared it so that I would understand that healing could come from "not" talking about something, the same as it can come from forcing the conversation. She wanted me to know that forgiving with your whole heart heals wounds for both yourself and the person you are forgiving, even if they don't know it. She also wanted me to know that we can choose joy if we want too, no matter what. She chose joy. My dad also chose joy. Most of my parents' relationship was filled with love, faith, joy, laughter, and lots of pranks; more on this later!

Everyone loved both my parents. I think my sister even said she used to think she was popular until she realized that her friends just wanted to hang out at our place with the family. I had an ex-boyfriend take his fiancé over to meet my parents; talk about awkward, but that is how my parents affected others. They brought joy to all that came in contact with them.

Step 1 – Your Base: Take a few minutes and describe your parents (and your spouse's parents if there are two of you), what you remember about your parents, what you liked about your childhood, and what you would have changed.

# Chapter 2

# Adding Kids to the Mix!

Twenty years of kids to be exact!

My sister, Lorie, was born first, when my mom was twenty and my dad was twenty-one. She was the first of the "adding kids to the gang." I don't think she was planned, but she was welcomed! She inherited my mom's strength for sure.

The second was Becky, and I know that there were health issues with Becky that broke my mom's heart. She had her little family to fill her heart back up, and God helped to mend that break. My mom talks about the challenges of helping Becky heal and how much struggle there was in their relationship from the pain of helping Becky heal. Things are not always easy, and in this case, they were downright painful. No mother should ever have to go through this, and no child should ever have to heal through pain, but it was better than the alternative. Even with all the health challenges, Becky has my mom's kindness.

Timothy was next up, and my mom and Timothy almost died (I think). My mom's blood and Timothy's blood were not compatible, and again, this is just my memory, or lack thereof, of stories I heard growing up. Tim was tiny for his age, and he is my dad's son. He is the prankster that follows in my dad's footsteps, as I can attest too!

These three were (and still are), the "older" kids, the first family. They have a different perspective of life as a Morehouse than the younger family. Their camping trips were VW beetles, tents, tarps and the "really not so well off financially" batch of kids. But what they didn't have in money, they had in love and fun. I know I am still jealous I was not part of the "Pineville" house water fight. Yes, you read that right, a water fight, inside and outside, involving hoses, buckets, and lots of cleaning up after, but this is a cherished story that I missed out on because I wasn't born yet. It is the Holy Grail of stories!

After moving into the Haines Canyon house, I came along. I am ten years younger than my brother and the start of the "younger" kids, the second family. Yes, I was a mistake, and I am sure with the number of pranks I played on my mom, she remembers this, maybe not so fondly sometimes. I also am my father's daughter. If my brother is prankster one, I am prankster two.

I was my brother's little sister and my dad's daughter. I studied them. I watched how they planned and executed the pranks. I knew I had to be better than both of them and, especially, better than Timothy. Heck, he was ten years older than me; I was at a complete disadvantage.

Lorie, being 15 years older than me, started working in downtown Los Angeles and decided to bring home these small jigsaw puzzles for me to work. I could work them in no time. This just inspired her to get harder puzzles. I am not sure how much of her paycheck she spent on these amazing puzzles, but I loved every one of them. While she endeavored to find the one I could not work, I knew I could work anything she brought to me. These were cherished memories for me.

Becky, being 13 years older than me, has a special memory for me when she got her first car, a '55 VW beetle. She took me to the drive in to see "Herbie the Love Bug" when it came out. I remember that movie and seeing it with Becky in the beetle like it was yesterday.

Timothy is my big brother. He and I were partners in crime. He was the best at setting up "situations" that would usually have an outcome of a very successful prank. Things from water dumping on people's heads (usually my dad coming home from work), to the sprayer in the kitchen being set so that the next person to turn on the kitchen faucet got a shower. He has a special place in my heart for teaching me how to laugh. We were eating at a diner once and saw Lorie and her best friend walking in to the "to go" counter. Timothy and I grabbed some fries, snuck up behind them, knocked their knees out from them and dropped the fries down their backs ... typical Morehouse style, only to discover it wasn't my sister and her friend, I don't think I have ever laughed that hard. Thankfully, they were understanding.

I was blessed to have the amazing "older" kids as my guides growing up.

Staci was born just short of twenty years after Lorie was born. Staci had the unfortunate honor of being the one I could practice my pranks and teasing on. I was not kind to Staci, and on more than one occasion, I was in trouble for picking on her. In many ways, Staci is the one that would run circles around me, and I think I ended up a number of times doing her chores because of it. My favorite came when she bet me she could do the Rubik's Cube before I could go feed the horses and get back. Challenge accepted; that cube was hard! I ran down the hill, doled the hay out to the horses, fed and locked up the chickens, made sure all the water troughs were full, and ran back up to the house. Lo and behold, there sat the cube, looking just like it did when we bought it. I was crushed. How could my little sister do something in 20 minutes that I could not do at all? It was years later that she confessed she just took the little cubes off and stuck them back on the right places. She takes the cake for pranks of all time! I am still laughing at that one!

This was the Morehouse gang.

# Chapter 3

# What are the Keys to a Happy Family?

The key to every lock is designed specifically for that lock.

My mom and dad designed their family, not by intention, but by love and laughter. Our family had our needs met, we were filled with joy, we enjoyed a peaceful home and a fun life.

**You get to design your family!**

What are the keys that make up your ideal family? As you read this book, picture the things that resonate with you, jot down some notes of things you can add to your family. My purpose for writing this book is to share some ideas on parenting that made my family an amazing place to grow up.

Here are the keys that defined our family:

- ❖ Love
- ❖ Laughter
- ❖ Peace

## Love

This, by far, was the biggest key. I remember seeing my parents holding hands and knowing that I wanted to have someone to hold hands with for the rest of my life. I could see how much they loved each other, even with the practical jokes and the tough times; their love was a beacon to all that came in contact with them.

Love was all around us as kids. My parents showed us love with hugs, holding our hands, and, most of all, making us know we were important. Even when it was something simple, like the ice cream truck coming by, they always had money set aside so that we could get a treat. I cherish the memories of my favorite, the orange sherbet push up that was my treat of choice. It still makes my mouth water thinking about it. We would be swimming and hear the familiar song playing from the ice cream truck. We would jump out of the pool and rush to the side of the road, where mom would meet us with the money to pay for our precious treats. We would sit by the side of the pool and relish the sweet, cold deliciousness.

I knew I was loved by how hard my mom worked, doing laundry, cleaning, polishing, keeping things looking nice for us. My mom had one or two jobs at most times, along with taking care of all of us and the home. I knew I was loved by my dad working hard for our family and including us in the fun at work. He would take me to work with him, and I would get to clean the machines in the machine shop he owned.

I knew I was loved by my sisters and brother. I remember the hour drive to and from the sailboat; my brother would make sure I

17

enjoyed all of the drive time, pretending to operate on me and pull fun things out of my belly while we laughed hysterically. We would play driving games (before the age of electronics, we would make up games to play). He would take me sailing out on the dinghy, just the two of us. All of us played games of all kinds!

## Laughter

There are some keys to laughter:

- ❖ Anything is fair game, unless someone is really hurt.
- ❖ It is okay to have stuff come out your nose if you laugh really hard.
- ❖ It is perfectly acceptable to make others laugh.
- ❖ Learn to laugh at yourself.

I think, more than anything, laughter is what kept our family together. Even now, 50 years later, we can get together and laugh hysterically about something that happened during those childhood years. One of us will think of something and mention it, and we all burst out in hysterics. We can laugh at present day stuff too. I think the laughter, and learning to laugh, is a true gift. I had a friend tell me once, "Elise, it isn't that what happens to you is funny; it is that you think it is funny." This is so true; it is all about how you look at life. Can you find the funny in what is happening? My family is gifted in finding the funny. It is a skill that everyone should learn! Jot that one down.

Sometimes, things had to be turned around to make them funny. I remember getting hurt; I banged my elbow, the not-so-funny funny bone. I was crying, and my dad stomped gently on my foot and said, "Now your elbow doesn't hurt, does it?" At that point, we would all crack up! It wasn't about not having stuff happen; it was all about turning it around into something that we could laugh about.

Where we grew up, there were wild fires every summer and fall. We would prepare with putting trash cans of water on the roof so that

19

my dad and brother could go up on the roof and use the water to put out embers if they landed on the roof. One day, my dad said for me to go get the camera and take a picture of my sister, Becky, and cousin, Barb, as they were lying out in the sun on the patio. He was going to go up on the roof and dump the trash can of water on them while I took the picture! Brilliant prank! I got all set up and had them posing for a stylish picture, and I captured it perfectly when the water was about 6 inches above their head. What we didn't think of was that with the water on the roof, it was hot water. This was a prank gone awry, but still to this day, to me, it was funny.

It was all about learning to laugh.

## Peace

While there was a lot of joking and pranks, I always felt that we had a peaceful home.

What made up a peaceful home for me?

Prayer, time, and choices to keep us busy.

Prayer: God was part of our family, not just on Sundays, but every day. We prayed on our own, and we prayed as a family. I was encouraged to get up early, ride my horse up into the mountains, and watch the sunrise. It was my time with God, on a mountain, with the sun rising and the rays washing over me. I would then have to race home, shower and get to school, but the personal time with God, in those early morning hours, was precious to me. I was encouraged to find my path to God, my path to prayer.

Time: We had time to ourselves, time together as a family, and time with family and friends. Time was valued, which brought about peace. There are so many amazing memories of family time, but I think the most precious for me was my dad leaving his work and coming home for dinner, even if he had to go back to work. He was there for dinner time.

The time my mom gave to me was also precious. My mom used to get up in the early morning to help me bathe horses and hold them while I braided their manes for competition. She wasn't even a fan of horses, but this was just one example of how she gave her time to me, and it was a gift that changed the course of my life. It showed me that I can also give time to those that I love, even when it isn't convenient. It is remembered and cherished.

Choices to keep us busy: I think a big part of this peace was being busy. Chores were expected, and while not always done right, they were done, and our allowances depended on us completing them. We played games as a family, Yahtzee, cards, board games and even Solitaire if you didn't have anyone to play with. We played in the yard, hiked in the mountains, rode horses, swam, and sailed on most weekends. We could lay by the fish pond and just immerse ourselves in watching the fish and frogs. We went to the library once a week and always had books we were reading. Our time was filled, and we had so many choices of things to do, I was never bored, I was never depressed, I had choices.

If I sit down and really look at the peaceful lives we had, the memories come flooding back.

All of this made for a peaceful home.

## Now it is your turn.

Step 2 – Think about what three keys would be amazing for your family. If you could have that perfect family, what words would you use to describe it?

These words will be used later in the book, so you may want to put them on a bookmark or a sticky note!

Here are a few that come to mind and to help get you started:

- ❖ Joyful
- ❖ Humorous
- ❖ Happy
- ❖ Strong
- ❖ Resilient
- ❖ Peaceful

- ❖ Affectionate
- ❖ Devoted
- ❖ Healthy
- ❖ Loving
- ❖ Nurturing
- ❖ Influential

# Chapter 4

# Create Your Ideal Family

The right ingredients will make the family!

* ❖ Health
* ❖ Knowledge
* ❖ Experience

## What makes up the health of a family?

The obvious answer is physical health. This is different for every person and every family. I know when I was about 5, I wanted to play a board game with some of my relatives, and they declined, saying they couldn't sit on the floor long enough to play a board game. It so deeply affected me, I vowed that I would never let that happen to me. When I got older, I wanted to be able to play games with the kids on the floor. Now, it wasn't that big of a deal; we picked up the game and moved it to the table, but that was a defining moment in my little life about health. My family is healthy. There are bits and pieces here and there that maybe were not healthy, but I don't remember anything specific. Health is so important to happiness; they go hand in hand.

What about mental health? I would not have thought of this as a kid, but looking back, it was so important. We were balanced mentally. I didn't even know what anger was until I was older, and the experience of anger was shocking to me. We had love, laughter, joy, fun, and even when the times were tough, we always just had the feeling that God would provide. It wasn't that we didn't feel sadness or stress, but the hope and joy would just bounce right back into our lives. What I really learned about mental health growing up were a few things:

- ❖ Happiness is a practice. I learned to be happy and joyful.
- ❖ Laughter can make things better that are otherwise not so pleasant.
- ❖ If I was feeling under the weather or stressed or had feelings that were not pleasant, people didn't enjoy being around me. If I was feeling good and being joyful, people enjoyed being around me. It wasn't that I couldn't have feelings like that; it was that those feelings were processed alone, on my own.
- ❖ Feeling good and enjoying life is a choice.

## Knowledge

My parents didn't "know" how to be parents; they knew how to be friends, best friends. They designed the parenting part as they went. When challenges would come up, they would tackle the challenges with prayer, fortitude, and a desire for the outcome to be fun. This clear direction led them to design the family life that they wanted.

There was always a knowing that God would provide. This was a key to reducing or eliminating stress. Stress is a large factor in unhappy families. By knowing that there was a greater purpose, a divine guidance, the stress melted away. Faith and trust kept the doors and windows opening for the future of our family.

One of the precious times we had when we had to fully trust and rely on our knowledge was a Friday evening after work, sailing to Catalina for the weekend. We made this trip seven or eight times every summer, and on this particular trip, when we left Los Angeles harbor, we could see the fog bank rolling in. We made sure the compass heading was on track, got the radar reflector up the mast, and had the fog horn on standby. As we sailed into that fog bank, we had to trust, we had to rely on our knowledge, and we had to stay the course. The fog was so dense, I could not see my hand in front of my face. I was in charge of the fog horn. Once a minute, I had to blow the horn. My dad was sailing the boat and keeping the boat on the heading for the Isthmus Cove on Catalina Island.

At one point, we could hear a cargo ship going by. All of a sudden, in the dense fog, we heard FIVE blasts. That means someone was in front of the ship. We had no idea if it was us, but it sounded a little further off than where we were. We stayed the course and came out of the fog just as we arrived at Catalina. Our friends that had left Los Angeles about the same times as us did not arrive.

We found out later that they were so close to the ship, they could feel the beat of the giant props, and so they decided to turn around and go back. They sailed over the next morning after the fog had lifted. In both cases, knowledge was critical to the success of the voyage to the island.

I remember this trip as one of courage, one of pulling together as a family to accomplish a goal. We were all praying. It was scary but also powerful. We knew we were prepared, and we knew we were in God's hands. We made the journey many times in the fog, but this trip was one we would talk about and remember at family get togethers.

This has been a metaphor for so much in our family and in our life. None of us ever know what tomorrow will bring or even what could happen in the next minute. We have knowledge to guide us along our path, we have knowledge to make adjustments when needed, and we have the knowledge to enjoy our lives and our families, if we choose to.

## Experience

You can study and read and learn as much as you want, but until you actually practice it, it is not reality. My parents practiced parenting. This really hit me while I was writing this book. They would try things, see what worked and what didn't work and make adjustments. Each kid was different, and what worked for one didn't necessarily work for the others. We all grew up individuals, happy and blessed.

When I talk about making adjustments, there was a vision that guided those adjustments. They wanted a happy, healthy family. Each person was a member of the family but also an individual. My mom would go with what she thought would work in any situation, and then, if it didn't work, she would adjust and always keep in mind the end vision. I am sure, about now, you are asking how in the world do you do this?

There's one example of this that's stuck with me through all these years for adjusting to get the end result instead of forcing things. My family ate dinner together. It was our time of joy, storytelling, laughter and refueling our bodies. This also meant that we ate what was put on our plates in front of us. When Staci came along, she had a preference for peanut butter sandwiches for dinner, and it was a struggle for her to eat what was on our plates at dinner. My dad would be upset about her not eating, and it would just put that layer of stress on the meal. There were options for how to solve the issue, but what my mom did was just a great example of looking at the situation, looking at the vision of a happy family, and making the adjustment.

My mom started giving Staci her sandwiches before dinner time. Guess what? Happy family dinner time! Sometimes, Staci would sit with us and enjoy all the company and family talk, but the stress was gone. It wasn't ideal, it wasn't the original picture, but from experience, it worked. It was an adjustment to the original picture to get the desired outcome. I think so many times, rules are put in place and never adjusted to reach the ultimate vision when necessary.

Our dinners went back to laughter, to sharing stories, and to all the practical jokes that went on at dinner time.

# Part 2

# Do you have a "Healthy" family

# Chapter 5

# Wouldn't it be Nice if We Could Wave a Magic Wand and be Healthy?

How was it growing up?

My family is healthy. In general, we didn't have lots of issues to deal with, but there were things that we did that I believe kept us healthy to some degree.

Looking up at my brother, sisters, and parents, as a kid, I saw them being active. There wasn't a lot of time in front of the TV or sitting on the couch. We were always "doing" stuff, fun or chores. I must say, I preferred the fun, but both kept us active and fit.

On the weekends, we would go sailing, not on a boat with a wheel, but on a boat with a tiller. Let me just say, holding the tiller (a wooden arm linked to the rudder) while bracing my feet on the opposite side of the cockpit, heeled over (tipping from the wind), pulling with all my strength to keep the boat on a straight course while the wind and waves are pushing in opposite directions and against the rudder was not only exhilarating; it was exhausting.

Hoisting the sails to the top of the mast required pulling down like climbing a rope in school, only your feet stayed on the boat and the sail went up. Tacking (changing direction) was always a challenge to pull the sail over to the other side of the boat at the right speed to time with the bow (front of the boat) coming around to the new direction. When driven by the wind, and the changes in the wind direction, all of this was not only technical, it was physical. We slept well after a great day sailing.

Physical health didn't just come from activities like sailing, it also came from laughter. I know the saying, "laughter is the best medicine," has been around for a long time, but in so many ways, it is true. I remember my sides and my abs hurting from laughter many times every day. It was better than sit ups or crunches, in my mind. Laughter got our hearts worked up too and our breathing. You have to breathe really deep when laughing, to the point of not being able to catch your breath. This was regular for our family.

One of the greatest stressors I see in families around me that keeps them from laughing together is exhaustion. Kids not going to bed, kids not sleeping through the night, and other things that keep sleep from being rejuvenating as it was designed to be.

My parents had the right idea on bedtimes that helped us grow up listening to our bodies. From an early age, they would say that yawning was a sign that it was time to go to bed and get some sleep. Everyone knows that yawns are contagious, and they would start yawning about twenty minutes before bedtime. Of course, we would start yawing too, and in just a few minutes, we would pick up what we had been doing, go in and brush our teeth and change into our pajamas and crawl into bed, calling for them to come tuck us in. This was brilliant in several ways. It was the start of teaching us to listen to our bodies and do what was good for our health, and it got enough sleep for everyone in the family.

There was only one real challenge with it. I used to get up really early in the morning and ride my horse up into the mountains to watch the sunrise before school. Well, by three o'clock, I would be starting to yawn. I would go crawl into bed if my mom didn't watch me like a hawk. I would sleep so soundly that they couldn't wake me up, and on a number of occasions, I missed dinner completely. I still do not have any problem sleeping, and I wonder how much learning to listen to my body has helped with deep, sound sleep.

Exhaustion can also come from work situations and pressures. I loved that my dad took a break from work to come home and have dinner and laugh, and I believe that break gave him the second wind so that the work didn't become exhausting.

## How has society changed now in general?

I see a huge change from when I was younger. We played outside and inside, the whole family, regularly. We rode Pogo sticks, rode horses, went sailing, hiking, swimming, had pillow fights, and played hide and go seek, tag, kick the can, and as many things as we could think up. We played card games and board games and many other games. Now, I look around, and kids are still, sitting with their electronics or screen of some sort. Maybe not all kids, and maybe not all the time, but much more than we ever did. I see parents that don't have the time or the energy to just play with their kids regularly. I see parents glued to their screens and texting, emailing, etc. and not participating as part of a family. I see a society that is becoming settled, still, giving up activity and movement.

We watched TV 30 minutes a day when I was young. That was the only screen time we had. The rest of the time was reading, homework, and play, lots and lots of play. The memories I have of childhood are so fulfilling and happy. When I even start to feel overwhelmed, I go back and fill up with that joy, like a battery charger.

## What would I have changed?

If I could have changed anything physically about my childhood, it might have been learning to eat healthier. I have learned a lot about healthy eating as an adult. We ate very well for the times, but now, I look back and would not have had as much sugar or bread products. Instead, I would have had more salads and natural sweeteners. I would have enjoyed more tea and less soda. At this point, I really wish we came with owner's manuals for our bodies!

I do not believe we were designed to become obese, have arthritis and pain, and age hurting. I believe that is being caused by what we eat to some degree.

Step 3 – Physical Health Inventory

- ❖ How is your family physically?
- ❖ Kids?
- ❖ Parents?
- ❖ What changes could be made to improve your family health?

# Chapter 6

# Joy and Laughter Go Hand in Hand!

How much is emotional health created vs. inherited?

### Parents' Emotional Health

I have thought about the above question a lot. Is emotional health created or is it inherited. Let's just take a look at my parents. Their parents were hard workers and supported their families, but there was also a lot of struggle and stress. My dad's mom would sneak out at night when she was younger and go partying in down town Los Angeles in the roaring twenties. I know she had an affinity for drinking and smoking because that was still part of her life when I was little. I don't know a lot of details about my grandparents, but let's just say there were challenges for sure. I already shared a little about my mom's parents and their struggles and grace.

My mom and dad were very different emotionally from their parents, from what I could tell. My mom and dad laughed! They found things to laugh at and created an atmosphere of joy. Their friends, and our friends for that matter, flocked to be around my parents. I do not believe any of that was inherited; I truly believe it was created. To me, this is great news!

Let's just look at this for a moment. If joy and laughter are created, then it doesn't matter where you are at right now, in this moment; it only matters that you choose joy and laughter. (You can substitute your key words from step 2, if they are different than joy and laughter.) If you think about each day as a blank canvas, and you get to paint that canvas for that day, you can choose your colors, your paint brushes, your picture. You can choose your world to look and feel like your words.

My parents painted their picture each and every day. My dad would push my mom out of bed so she could go make everyone's lunches, and they would giggle about it. They would have breakfast together, and then my dad would go off to the machine shop we owned, and my mom would go off to what she was involved in for that day – 20 years as a preschool teacher and then working at the shop for many years with my dad. At lunch time, they would sit at their desks at the machine shop, share their lunch, and play a game of cards together. If there weren't any immediate practical jokes in the works, there was sure to be one or two over the afternoon. Mom would come home and prepare dinner, and we would set the table. Then, my dad would show up, usually having some practical joke played on him coming home; half the time, he would spot it, half the time, we would "get" him. All of this led to laughter.

Dinner was the best, as I explained previously. After dinner, it was all about the games. If my dad had to go back to work, it was the rest of us, but he would try and get work done so we could all play. I remember my grandma and other relatives coming over and all of us sitting down to a mad game of Yahtzee. My grandma would get so excited and yell, "Yahtzee," and we would all laugh. Then, us kids were off to bed, and my parents could finish painting their picture for that day, which I was not privy too, but I know it was amazing by the joy that they showed the next morning.

I am sure there were challenges, but the joy and laughter far outweighed them. I think it was a practice - a practice to look at the bright side of things and a practice to enjoy life as it came. My parents showed us that emotional side of things.

## Kids' Emotional Health

This is where I come in. There are so many lessons I learned about emotions as I grew up. My first emotional memory was a day when I came out of my room and made the statement that I was bored. My mom looked at me with a quizzical look on her face that I remember clearly, and she said, "You have a room full of things to do, a yard full of things to do, and you have the choice to be bored or enjoy all the things you have." She just turned around and went back to what she was doing. That was powerful, life defining for me. We have so much in our lives to enjoy; we should just get busy enjoying them.

One day, a friend and I decided we wanted to know what it felt like to get in trouble. We were good kids and never got in trouble. We wanted to know what kids felt like that got into trouble. We decided to turn my bedroom upside down, literally. We emptied all the drawers, took everything off the bed, and piled the entire room up in the middle of the floor in a huge pile. My mom wondered why we were so quiet and opened the door to check in on us. We knew we were in big trouble. She looked at us and said, "Wow, it looks like you are having a great time; be sure and clean up when you are done playing." That was so powerful. We were crushed, deflated, but I remember thinking that we had a really good time, and getting in trouble wasn't worth the effort of not only ripping the room apart but having to put it all back together. My mom later admitted that she had to completely redo everything we had done, but she found so much joy in the mess we had made because of the fun we had.

The other really powerful lesson on emotion that they taught me was about anger. One day, when I was angry (I don't even remember

43

what I was angry about), I came out to the front room in a complete snit, and my mom just kindly said, "We really don't want to be around someone that is in a huff; if you want to be angry, can you please go outside or go into your room, and you can be as angry as you want. When you feel happy again, you are welcome to come back out here and join us." Again, with her wisdom, my emotions were not bad; in fact, they seemed perfectly normal, but it just made me really think whether I wanted to be angry and alone or happy and playing games with others – my choice. Was being angry worth it? I remember this lesson clearly, but to this day, I have no idea what I was angry about. How many times do we let anger take over, but really, the choice for happiness would be so much more rewarding?

My whole family laughs, loves, cries, and shares all the emotions together, as a family. There is no holding in emotions; we let them all out as they come. My family cries together for joy or sorrow. I remember when the orthodontist told me I had to have two teeth pulled for my braces, my dad cried, right there in the office with me. It was okay to show tears.

Is there an emotional area that needs improvement in your family? Do you hold in emotions or let them be expressed? Do you use emotions for lessons or just shut them down? This is a great area to really look at emotions – are they real or perceived, flowing or dammed up?

## Step 4 – Emotional Inventory

- ❖ What is your emotional inventory?
- ❖ What is your family's emotional inventory?
- ❖ Are there changes that can be made?

# Chapter 7

# Our Faith Was Strong

## God Will Provide!

### Faith

I learned so many lessons about faith. When I was young, two or maybe three years old, I was horse crazy. I guess I was born horse crazy from the stories. My mom said that when I was a year old, they couldn't get me off the carousel and had to pry my hands off the horse and hold them so they could get me off the horse. My mom finally relented and said, "When you can afford a horse, you can have a horse." Note to other parents: this was a great thing for me but maybe not so good for my parents. First thing I learned to read was the newspaper classified ads. The second thing I learned was how to count money and earn money. I also learned how to save money. These were great lessons for my entire life. It wasn't long before we had a pony in the yard. My mom never admitted that she regretted telling me that, and she held to her word; I had my pony. For me, the prayers that I said every night for my pony and the ability to have that dream come true were linked to the phrase that I heard a lot, "God will provide." I realized that there was a power to pray, but that power also needed action on my part to allow the prayer to be answered.

While prayers were answered and we recognized them and said our prayers of thanksgiving, there were times at church that things didn't go as planned, and we raised a joyful noise unto the Lord ... usually not at the right times. There was a day when Staci said she was going to sneeze, and so my mom dug a handkerchief out of her purse and handed it across me to Staci, and just as she reached across, I sneezed, right onto her arm. We all cracked up and excused ourselves from church. There was another time that I had an ant on my leg, and I figured out that it was like those little cars that you wound up and they would change directions as they bumped into things. Every time I put my finger in front of the ant, it changed directions. My dad was watching me play with the ant, and then, all of a sudden, it just fell over dead. Again, we all cracked up and excused ourselves from church. This happened on most Sundays, at least in my memory.

We enjoyed wonderful times at church and with our church family. What stands out for me as a child was that faith wasn't just on Sundays. It was just a way of life for our family. God's creations are all around us if we open our eyes, listen with our ears, touch with our hands, smell and taste as well. God gives us so much to wonder about, to enjoy.

God was an integral part of our family, right there with us, day in and day out. He was in our surroundings, the colors of our lives. We were thankful and practiced gratitude as a family and as individuals. I mean, getting a pony really brought the meaning of the word grateful to a whole new level of feeling it. These were all learning experiences in faith that have been with me every day of my life, and

I think they guide me to just flow along, day to day, in joy, even as an adult, looking for God's grace around me and in all that I do.

Step 5 – Challenge for you (if faith is a part of your family):

- ❖ What areas of faith are your strengths as a family?
- ❖ What areas of faith could be strengthened as a family?

# Part 3

# Knowledge - How do you get the family you want?

# Chapter 8

# Paint the Picture of Your Dream Family

Involve everyone in what the family will look like!

My parents had a great way of including everyone in the picture of our family and our plans. We would get to pick where we were going camping or on vacation. We took a trip across the country in 1976 that made people just stop in shock. We were gone for three weeks and had ten people in a 25-foot motorhome (more to come on this later) for over a week of that trip. The best part was we all had a blast. It was the trip of a lifetime. We planned the trip through AAA, and each day, we would pick the top sights to see and vote on them. While driving, the rest of us were playing card games or board games. We had to go to bed in the right order and get up in the right order and pray we didn't have to get up in the middle of the night.

This trip was an amazing example of how much our family just loved life. I would hear all the naysayers before we left saying that it would be horrible and then all the disbelievers when we arrived back home that couldn't believe we were able to enjoy it. There was not a single fight or angry word. It was laughter and fun that we all talk about to this day.

Whether or not we openly realized it, our family vision was to enjoy life. This was the guiding light that we followed through the years. This vision made the solutions pop up in front of us and made decisions clear. A great example of this was our camping. We had tents and we had campers, but with the size of our family, why not a motorhome (besides the fact that they were way out of the income limits set by owning our own machine shop)?

My uncle, my dad's brother, was co-owner of the machine shop and had three boys. When the two families got together, they figured out a way to have a motorhome to enjoy for both families. Why not share the motorhome, and why not have others buy it for us? Like I said, vision is so important to guide the direction of the family. We decided to purchase a motorhome, as a rental. Each family would get three weeks every other year; the rest of the year, it would be available to rent to other families that couldn't afford to purchase a motorhome. When it wasn't rented, either family could use it for long weekends. This was a great example of how to bring joy into a family that barely got by week to week.

It wasn't always about what was best for the whole family; sometimes, it was about what was best for one member of the family. This story is about me, and everything about this is precious to me, and I am so grateful for my amazing parents. I loved horses, and they were part of my life, as I have explained, from a very young age. When I turned fourteen, my friend invited me to go watch a jumper show with her. When my mom saw my eyes light up watching those gorgeous big horses sailing over the jumps, she knew we were in for a change in direction. My friend was taking lessons at a great place about seven miles or so from our house. I started riding my horse to take lessons and then riding home after. It wasn't the best riding with having to ride on some major roads and crossing a lot of intersections in the suburbs of Los Angeles.

After a few months, my parents decided to move closer to where I was taking lessons. It was a hard decision and one that was a huge sacrifice for everyone else in the family. The home we were leaving had character, it had a pool, and it was right at the base of the Angeles National Forest. The home we moved into had almost zero character, no pool, an amazing view, and located less than a mile from where I took lessons. I was on my way to being a hunter/jumper/equitation rider! The family adjusted to support the dreams of their child. The rest of our lives stayed the same – practical jokes run amuck, laughter through dinner, games at all times of the day and night, and the addition of being able to ride to my lessons safely, which was less stress on my mom and more time for me to finish my homework.

Imagine what a family can accomplish if they put their minds together, their hearts together, and figure out how to bring joy into their lives, the family and the individuals, each and every day.

Step 6 – Sit down and have a family gathering and discuss your family vision. Here are a few things to get you started:

- ❖ What does the family want the vision of the future to look like?
- ❖ How far off from this vision is the family today?
- ❖ What is the big dream for each person in the family?
- ❖ What can be done to start working towards those dreams – family and individual?
- ❖ How can you make the economics of the dreams work?

# Chapter 9

# Life Lessons

Consequences are real.

How many lessons do children learn from their parents and their family? How many lessons do the parents learn from their kids?

My parents had a true gift of letting us learn life lessons.

**Let the Mistake Happen, See the Consequences:**

I am sure it is hard for parents to just let the mistake happen and then let the child experience the consequences. In the story earlier, where my friend and I were trying to get in trouble, we made a mistake, and my mom let us have the consequences without putting in the emotion of anger. I know parents that would have been angry to open up that door and see the whole room in chaos. Their reaction would have been anger. My mom's reaction was calm and reassuring. After she left the room, I am sure there was a lot of laughter as she went about getting ready for dinner. We learned the lesson, we committed the mistake, and we suffered the consequences of having to put the whole room back together and having to deal with the disappointment of, once again, not being in trouble.

Another mistake that I made when I was young was very creative but also had some consequences. I had found that a great place to hide veggies that disagreed with me was in my baked potato skin. Since I was usually the one that had to do dishes from too much laughter, it was a great way to get out of actually eating veggies. One night, after I had gone to bed, my mom found the veggies in the trash can. She woke me up and asked me if I had thrown my veggies away in my potato skin. I made the ultimate mistake. I said no. I am not sure what the consequence would have been if I had not lied, but the lie was the mistake I was punished for. She used the opportunity to let me see the consequences of telling a lie. I had to eat an entire plate of vegetables in twenty minutes. For every one left on my plate at the end of twenty minutes, I would get a spanking. I did end up with quite a few spankings. There was never a big deal made out of hiding the veggies, but there was a big deal made about lying that stuck with me. The mistake I made led to the consequence. Once again, there was no anger; it was just calm, reassuring to my young soul. I made the mistake, and I suffered the consequences.

## Laughter Makes All Things Better:

While talking about consequences, this was a really good one. We were out sailing with friends, and I was upset at my mom for something. I had my best friend there with me and wanted to show off that I was upset, so I stuck my tongue out at my mom. What I hadn't realized was that my dad was right behind me and saw me stick my tongue out. Here is where the mistake led to consequences. He washed my mouth out with soap. How could laughter possibly make that better? I made up my mind that I was not going to let my dad know how horrendous that soap tasted. So I smiled and laughed and said, "Wow, that tasted just like candy!" My dad looked at me laughing and stuck the soap in his mouth. Good thing my family laughs about everything because that bar of soap was nasty! He was so proud of me for sticking it to him that we all laughed, and we still laugh about that to this day.

My parents also taught us that laughter helps the pain go away. There isn't room for pain when we are all laughing our heads off. The biggest thing for me was when I would get hurt. I would bang my funny bone (which isn't funny) on a door frame and be in agony. My dad would see this and lightly stomp on my foot, and say, "Now your elbow doesn't hurt anymore, does it," as I would be hopping around on one foot. We would all have a good belly laugh. It was true, my elbow didn't hurt when my foot did. This had good points and not-so-good points. There are so many times when I see things happen, but I see it as a cartoon and laugh at really inappropriate times. It was a good habit to have and helped to evaluate how much pain you were really in.

Laughter seems to show up more when you look for laughter in your life. My mom had been really sick one summer and not able to go out of the house for several months. When she finally got the all clear, we went to our favorite restaurant for breakfast before church. There were about ten of us I think, and a bunch of us ordered pancakes. The waitress brought us a bunch of those little warm syrup pitchers, and as she was setting the plate down on the table, one fell off the edge and hit the table right in front of me. It hit at the exact right angle to soak me, head, face, top, lap, even my eyelashes wouldn't open properly. I had just taken my first (and hopefully last) syrup shower. There was a silhouette on the window behind me in syrup. The poor waitress looked like she had just seen a murder. The entire family, including me, burst out in full blown, belly shaking laughter. There were snorts we were laughing so hard. The waitress was shocked at our response, expecting anger and berating but witnessing the joy of a good situation. The lesson of laughter is one of the most important; laughter is a true gift. The more we can see the cartoon in the situation, the lighter the world becomes.

### Sticks and Stones Can Break My Bones but Words Will Never Hurt Me (Above All Else, Be Kind):

This was one of my mom's favorite sayings to help us through situations. As a kid, it really helped. It made things seem better as long as we actually weren't being beat up. As an adult, I realized that there should have been modifications to it. While I didn't have a lot of issues with people flinging words at me, I did fling words at Staci.

A group of us used to ride in Blue Shadows Mounted Drill Team, a horseback riding team, and on the drive to and from the stables with my riding friends with us, I was mean with words to Staci. There were a few street signs on the road that said "Dip in the Road," and I would yell out, "Staci, get out of the road!" I don't know if those words hurt her, but they hurt me when I look back at how mean I was. It took me a long time to forgive myself for saying those words as a kid (among other mean things I did). It was a great lesson for me to learn; while others' words, I could let roll off my back, when I was mean, those words hurt the person I said them to, and that, in turn, hurt me. I was not kind.

My mom taught me a valuable lesson but not in the way she intended. Looking back, this lesson would have been better as, "Above all else, be kind," the reverse of thinking about sticks and stones.

I think being kind is lost in a lot of families these days. With all the electronics and hiding behind screens, maybe it has taken away some of the emphasis on kindness. My family was kind in so many ways. We had a family down the street from us that wasn't that well off, and the kids were always welcome at our house for a dip in the pool and some hamburgers and hot dogs. This was just one example that stands out to me. The door was always open for those that needed a little kindness.

**Keep Trying Until You Get the Result You Want:**

This lesson was learned over time. It wasn't something that could be learned at one time. When I was struggling with homework, my dad would try and help me, but I would push back. I didn't know how to let him help me. But even though I struggled, both my mom and dad kept encouraging me to try, to rework it, to try different methods, to take a break and come back to it, but to keep at it until it was done. Through all the years, I had straight A's, and it was from this lesson.

Learning this lesson to keep trying started when I was young. I would go to the machine shop with my dad and "help" out. That was pretty funny looking back to when I was three or four and working in a machine shop. I would have the privilege of cleaning the machines. I would spray and wipe the machines as high as I could reach. I remember looking forward to growing, so I could just reach a little bit more of the machines since the bottom looked so nice where I could reach.

I see parents who don't have as much patience, and they jump in and finish up or take care of it, and that reduces the lesson dramatically. I know it must be hard for some, but for those that can let it be, it is a great learning experience for the kids. They see progress over time, and it encourages them to keep trying and to keep doing better.

One of the best lessons for me on this was playing Hide and Go Seek. I was always caught in the first thirty seconds of the game. I laughed. It didn't matter who I played with, I laughed. It didn't matter where I hid, I laughed. But I kept playing, and I knew that one day, I would figure it out.

Well, we were on one of our trips over at Catalina Island, and I was playing Hide and Go Seek with the big kids, the high school kids. I was probably ten or eleven. I finally gave up trying to hide and just went and sat on the wall with all the parents. The high school kids kept playing, but they didn't know I had quit. They searched and searched for me. Finally, they decided to give up and called, "Olly Olly Oxen Free" so that I would come out. This time, I had laughed and cracked up the whole time I had been hiding since I was in the middle of all the parents. I was sitting on the wall about two feet from the high school boy that called me free! It was the only game of Hide and Seek I ever made it to the end, but what a lesson to keep trying! I now had a method to play the game and not be caught immedietely.

## Look at the Bright Side:

This lesson was all from my mom. She was the queen of looking at the bright side and showing us how to do the same. When I look back, there are so many things that would have triggered anger in my friends and people that I know, but my mom taught us to see the other side of any situation.

My favorite was on the long trip across the country with all the family. We were stuck in traffic in New York City in a motorhome, and my mom, sitting in the passenger seat, looked over at us and said, "Well, the good news is we don't have to pay the money at the toll booths as fast." We all looked back at her and then cracked up. She took a sticky situation and made it okay.

When the huge Sylmar earthquake hit, it emptied all the cabinets in our kitchen into the middle of the kitchen floor. I remember the mess, and my mom just said, "Oh well, I was thinking of cleaning out and re-arranging the cupboards, and now seems like a good time." This was a huge mess, and I know I was so scared, but she made it not only normal, but she turned it around into the positive that was going to come out of it.

This is a skill that is learned. I know I learned it from my mom. It is a great way to go through life, and it keeps the emotions above the line; it takes away the anger and disappointment. It gives the ability to see the bright side, even when the situation isn't bright.

Step 7 – Life's Lessons

- ❖ What lessons do you want your kids to learn as they grow up?
- ❖ How can you create the situations for them to learn?

# Chapter 10

# The Elephant in the Room - Finances

Finances are built, one coin at a time.

Finances are not the topic anyone wants to talk about, but by talking about finances, things can change. My parents were never wealthy from a monetary perspective, but they were extremely blessed and wealthy from love and joy. There has to be a balance though between enjoying life and finances or there can be too much stress to enjoy life. Hiding the emotions and keeping the topic under wraps is the worst thing you can do. Being open, honest, and communicating short-term and long-term family plans is refreshing, and it guides the family.

Not too long after my parents were married, my dad, his brother, and a few others got together and started learning about retirement finances. My mom talked about the day my dad came home from the machine shop and told her that he and his brother were going to start investing in a retirement account. My mom was shocked and not too happy, but she listened to my dad, and he said it would be done before she ever saw the money, and she would never notice.

She was hesitant but jumped in with both feet to give it a try. My parents are in their 90s and still have an amazing life, with enough money to enjoy it. What a blessing that my dad learned about finances, discussed it with my mom, and they jumped in with both feet, committed to it and made it happen. They were able to enjoy life and save for retirement. Now, they are able to enjoy their retirement after enjoying their whole life.

The lesson here started with communication. The two of them talked through finances and learned together. They took a chance for their future and didn't sacrifice their joy of life. This took the stress out of finances, even though it wasn't much. They figured out how to make it work and still enjoy life.

When they first started the machine shop, there was fear. Taking a chance like that takes courage. My dad had been working for the phone company, my mom was raising three young children at home, and they had almost no savings (or none at all). My dad and his brother pooled their money and bought three pieces of equipment to start their own shop. My dad discovered that he was good with customers and the more complex machines, and my uncle was amazing at running the machine shop efficiently. Everyone had to watch their pennies to make ends meet, and there were others in the family that pitched in when they could to help out while they got the business up and running. I remember my grandma, my aunt, and my mom all pitching in to do the books. They used paper ledgers with debits and credits, and I remember looking up to them, knowing how to keep the business running and afloat financially. They did what they had to do, as a family and business owners. This business was the main source of income for two families, and my parents enjoyed the work and the income until they decided to retire and sell the business.

Another financial lesson I learned was that adjustments could be made as you go. My dad used to go to the yacht club board meetings all the time, and he would order something very inexpensive to watch our pennies. After the first few times, with everyone else ordering surf and turf, he realized they were just dividing the bill up at the end of the night evenly, so from then on, he ordered the surf and turf too and enjoyed a well-deserved meal from all his hard work. He would make up for this in other areas. This really stuck with me - to look at every situation with money and evaluate it, not with emotion, but with a sense of taking control, knowing what is being spent, how it is being spent, and what is being saved. My parents made sure that they didn't "save" for retirement at the "cost" of enjoying life. Think about this for a minute; let it soak in.

So many times, people save for retirement and then are too tired or not in good enough health to enjoy their retirement. My parents had an amazing balance throughout their life. I think it goes back to being kids in high school and keeping that feeling through the rest of their life. We "did" life - camping, hiking, swimming, sailing, rock hounding, gardening, building fish ponds, playing games, and so much more. There was an ease about our life, like floating down a river and just enjoying all of the scenery as it passes by. We didn't have the fancy boats or the fancy cars. Our home wasn't the largest, and our things were not the newest, shiniest, or the best. But the love we shared, the fun, the laughter, made us very wealthy, inside and out.

Step 8 – Financial target – Budgets

- ❖ What do you want your financial plan to look like?
- ❖ How can you involve the kids in the financial plan?

I like to think of jars that I learned from T. Harv Eker.  The jars I used when I first started were as follows:

- ❖ 10% - Charity
- ❖ 50% - Necessities
- ❖ 10% - Long term savings
- ❖ 10% - Education
- ❖ 10% - Fun
- ❖ 10% - Financial freedom (investments)

# Chapter 11

# Set the Family Course

Sailing to Catalina required setting a course; families with a course arrive at their destination.

One of the amazing things for our family was setting a course for the family. When I was young, my parents set the course for including sailing in our lives. This was a lifestyle, and it required lots of moving parts to all come together. We lived over an hour away from where we kept the sail boat in San Pedro.

Our first boat, Pawhee, was a wooden boat that came with something you never want to have out on the Pacific Ocean - leaks. That is what old wooden boats do; they leak. I am not sure how long we had Pawhee before we sold it and bought the 25-foot Coronado "Sea Drift." That boat was so much fun and the first boat we took back and forth so many weekends to Catalina Island. That boat had windows on the sides that would be under water, and us kids could stand down below and see under the ocean through the windows when we were sailing really hard. It was mesmerizing and what a great experience for parents and kids!

We sold Sea Drift and bought a 30-foot Coronado, "Sea Castle." This was when I really understood the vision that my parents had set forth for our sailing. They started saying their next boat would the "Sea Nile." That would be the boat they would retire with. They ended up retiring and selling Sea Castle, but the vision was still there, a beacon to our family through the years.

Sea Drift -> Sea Castle -> Sea Nile

How did this fit in with my dreams of riding? Again, individual dreams and family dreams were about meshing and making sure that everyone had the ability to make their dreams come true. We ended up sailing one weekend and then horse stuff the other weekend, alternating so that we got the sailing in and we also got my riding lessons and competitions fit in.

We set a course for our futures, too. I remember when I was five or six and figuring out what I could do as an adult to pay for my horses. We talked about the main things at that time. Veterinarian, nope, I pass out at the sight of blood. Lawyer, maybe. Engineer, this one I connected with, and it became my dream and my career. Doctor, nope, see veterinarian. I am sure a few other things were brought up, but I knew where I was heading, what I was doing, and why I was doing it. I had purpose. It helped me have a plan for not only getting the grades but also learning what I needed to learn. I had to plan how to pay for college and applied for and was awarded scholarships. I had a plan, and I executed that plan, and the family was always there supporting me.

When looking at setting the course for a family, there are many areas to consider, and all are important. So many times, the stress and financial issues or other issues take the lead in setting the course at the cost of happiness and joy.

Here are the areas that my family had as a course set for the future:

- ❖ Faith – Let God live in our lives.
- ❖ Financial – covering the needs of the family
- ❖ Health – emotional and physical
- ❖ Friendship – practical jokes, play
- ❖ Parenting – the lessons
- ❖ Friends and family – support and community

These are the guiding principles that my parents used to guide our family.

Step 9 – Set the Family Course

❖ What would you like your guiding principles to be for your family?

# Part 4

# Experience - Laughing Through Life

# Chapter 12

# Defined Boundaries

Would you want your neighbors using your kitchen?

Just imagine, it's Fourth of July weekend, and we are all swimming in the pool. My cousins are over, friends are visiting, we are all having a great time. All of a sudden, SPLASH, Woodstock, the neighbor's otter jumps into the pool to swim with us. We had so much fun and enjoyed having him in the pool with us. When my mom went in to the kitchen to get the fixings for the hamburgers and hot dogs, she came out of the house in fits of laughter. Woodstock had found his way into the kitchen at some point and helped himself to the hamburger buns! This brought fits of laughter to all of us but is also a great point on boundaries.

There were so many choices for the boundaries and outcomes in this afternoon. My mom could have been upset and disappointed, she could have been angry, but her natural reaction was to see the humor, the cartoon in the situation. Here we were having a great afternoon, and the neighbor, in the form of an otter, had joined us. It isn't every day that you get the chance to enjoy the company of an otter.  My mom had an amazing way of bringing laughter to boundaries that may have been invaded.

I think my dad was really creative in teaching us about boundaries, too.  I used to talk on the phone (before the days of our own cell phones, we had one family phone) for hours with my friends.  My dad wanted us to have family time and play games together, so he would take the extension of the phone and the kitchen timer - set to 15 minutes, and he would hide them somewhere together.  I would keep on talking with the ticking in our ears until at the 15-minute mark, it would go off and force us to hang up, so I could go find the timer and turn it off.  It was so much better than yelling at us all the time to "Get off the phone!"  It made the boundaries fun.

Now, boundaries between siblings were a completely different issue.  I had a date over once, and Staci wanted to hang out with us.  He happened to be a police explorer, so he had some handcuffs in his car.  We handcuffed her to the tether ball pole first.  She was able to pull off the top half of the pole and slide over the bottom half and return to hanging out with us.  We then handcuffed her to the mandarin tree, but she managed to slide her hand out of that one and show up again.  We finally realized we were just going to have to enjoy the company of younger sister Houdini.  We gave up and just let her stay.

Another great example of boundaries was on the sail boat. We were in close quarters with anywhere from four to eight of us on the boat. When it would get too much for my parents, they would put us out on the dinghy, tied off the back of the boat. As much as it would feel like a punishment, it was filled with amazing times. I remember lying on the edge of the dinghy and being able to see all the colorful fish. There were Sheepshead and Perch, Garibaldi and Bass. Leopard sharks were common and, once in a while, a Blue shark or even the one time while we were swimming, a Great White shark. The kelp beds would sway with the waves and looked like mermaid gardens all around us. These memories are still crystal clear and precious. What an amazing way to set boundaries and still have everyone happy to respect them.

Boundaries were always about the "how" can we get along together, not about how do we exclude people. It was a different way to look at things, and I don't think I realized this until much later in life. It was a blessing to look at boundaries in a way that was inclusive and supportive to all.

Step 10 – What do your family's boundaries look like?

- ❖ Do you need to improve your boundary system?
- ❖ Are your boundaries inclusive or exclusive?
- ❖ Are there areas parent -> child or child -> child that could be improved?
- ❖ Get together as a family and talk about your boundaries and how to improve them.

# Chapter 13

# Spend Time "Doing" Things

Put the electronics down and "BE" together, actively.

Now that you have your vision for your family, start doing.

There were so many weekends when I was growing up that my dad would get home from work on Friday and say, "Hey, let's head to the beach for the weekend," or he would say, "It is great weather; let's go up into the mountains and collect pine cones." With the campers, tents, sailboat, horses, and hiking all around us, we were always active, together as a family.

Activity doesn't have to be big things, or weekends; it can be the little things. We were at a restaurant, and my dad wanted to show us how you can "shoot" pens using the spring on the ink cartridge. The booths were really high, so it was just like a little rocket going up and coming down again somewhere on the table. We were fascinated until, all of a sudden, it went up, but it didn't come back down. We all looked at each other and then heard the lady behind us making crazy noises. My dad got up, trying really hard not to crack up, and said, "Excuse me, I am so sorry, my pen went on an adventure," and he picked it up and brought it back to our table while we were all in hysterics.

There were other times, while we were eating, that all of a sudden, one of us would disappear below the table as my dad would grab our feet with his feet and just pull us right under the table. If there were straws in paper, we certainly had the paper flying at someone while opening our straws. If you roll up the end a little bit into a ball before you shoot it, it flies better.

There were other little things as well. Rubber bands were a way of life for us, from wrapping one around the sprayer on the sink to the massive rubber band fights that were full scale war. One Christmas, I bought my brother and my dad each a six-shooter rubber band gun and a bag of rubber bands. I hid the bands with a bunch of clues, and you should have seen the two of them trying to get to their bag of bands first. It was a race of epic proportions.

If we were home, we were playing games of some sort. Card games and board games were a way of life. New Year's Eve was a casino party that even included a Craps table, and my uncle was the dealer. We worked jigsaw puzzles and played bumper pool.

Not all of this is for everyone and may even seem shocking to some but our family loved it.

Step 11 – Get Active

- ❖ What are three big things your family enjoys doing together?
- ❖ How can you incorporate those into each quarter or year?
- ❖ What are three little things your family enjoys doing together?
- ❖ How can you incorporate those into each week or month?

Talk about it, pick what would be amazing to do together, and be together. Talk while you are doing the activities. Set the phones down and look away from the screens. Don't participate in every organized sport available; decide to spend time together.

# Chapter 14

# Live a Life of Laughter

It takes a gift to see the world through the eyes of laughter.

Laughter can be learned. We learned about laughter every day. Some of my best memories are those things that brought laughter to the point of tears. Driving around was always sure to bring laughter. It didn't matter if we were going to the local store or driving across the country on vacation, laughter would bubble up, and we would find things to encourage that laughter. My mom would be running late, and she would go to put lipstick on in the car. My dad would wait until just the right moment and then just slightly swerve the wheel and see if he could mess her up. This would usually get a "TIM!", and then we would all crack up.

Grocery shopping was always an adventure. We would stand on the front of the shopping cart while my dad would race through the store like a NASCAR driver, and we would laugh and enjoy the ride. We had carts to take stuff from the car to the boat, and we would get rides in them with my dad acting like a drunk sailor and pretending to dump us into the water with us holding on for life! All of this would cause us to erupt in laughter. Nobody laughed more at this than my dad. I think most of the pranks were played so that he could have a great laugh.

My parents raised me to look for laughter. I realized as I got older that I wasn't laughing as much, I was letting life get to me instead of seeking the laughter. When I came to this realization with the pressures of life, I decided one New Year to make a major change instead of a resolution. I decided to attempt to laugh 400 laughs a day. This number was too big to track, and yet, it was big enough that I would search for things to see as funny, all day long. This was the gift my parents gave me on life perspective. Seek out the things that bring laughter. It will take situations that could bring anger and turn them around into laughter.

That old adage, "Laughter is the best medicine," has kept all of us healthy. My parents are in their nineties at the time of writing this, and they still share lots of laughter each and every day. It was a true blessing to be one of their kids.

Step 12 – Find ways to laugh together.

# Steps to Your Happy Family

Dream Big, Laugh Hard, Look for the Joy.

Step 1 – Your base: Describe your parents (and your spouse's parents, if there are two of you). What do you remember about your parents, what did you like about your childhood, and and what would you have changed?

Step 2 – Think about what three keys would be amazing for your family. If you could have that perfect family, what words would you use to describe it?

Here are a few that come to mind and to help get you started:

- ❖ Joyful
- ❖ Humorous
- ❖ Happy
- ❖ Strong
- ❖ Resilient
- ❖ Peaceful

- ❖ Affectionate
- ❖ Devoted
- ❖ Healthy
- ❖ Loving
- ❖ Nurturing
- ❖ Influential

Step 3 – Physical Health Inventory

- ❖ How is your family physically?
- ❖ Kids?
- ❖ Parents?
- ❖ What changes could be made to improve your family health?

Step 4 – Emotional Inventory

- ❖ What is your emotional inventory?
- ❖ What is your family's emotional inventory?
- ❖ Are there changes that can be made?

Step 5 - Challenge for you (if faith is a part of your family):

❖ What areas of faith are your strengths as a family?
❖ What areas of faith could be strengthened as a family?

Step 6 - Sit down and have a family gathering and discuss your family vision.  Here are a few things to get you started:

❖ What does the family want the vision of the future to look like?
❖ How far off from this vision is the family today?
❖ What is the big dream for each person in the family?
❖ What can be done to start working towards those dreams - family and individual?
❖ How can you make the economics of the dreams work?

## Step 7 – Life's Lessons

❖ What lessons do you want your kids to learn as they grow up?
❖ How can you create the situations for them to learn?

## Step 8 – Financial target – Budgets

❖ What do you want your financial plan to look like?
❖ How can you involve the kids in the financial plan?

I like to think of jars that I learned from T. Harv Eker. The jars I have used when I first started were as follows:

❖ 10% – Charity
❖ 50% – Necessities
❖ 10% – Long term savings
❖ 10% – Education
❖ 10% – Fun
❖ 10% – Financial freedom (investments)

Step 9 – Set the Family Course

❖ What would you like your guiding principles to be for your family?

Step 10 - What do your family's boundaries look like?

❖ Do you need to improve your boundary system?
❖ Are your boundaries inclusive or exclusive?
❖ Are there areas parent -> child or child -> child that could be improved?
❖ Get together as a family and talk about your boundaries and how to improve them.

Step 11 – Get Active

- ❖ What are three big things your family enjoys doing together?
- ❖ How can you incorporate those into each quarter or year?
- ❖ What are three little things your family enjoys doing together?
- ❖ How can you incorporate those into each week or month?

Talk about it, pick what would be amazing to do together, and be together. Talk while you are doing the activities. Set the phones down and look away from the screens. Don't participate in every organized sport available; decide to spend time together.

Step 12 – Find ways to laugh together.